To Be A WRITER

A GUIDE FOR YOUNG PEOPLE
WHO WANT TO WRITE AND PUBLISH

BARBARA SEULING

TWENTY-FIRST CENTURY BOOKS
A DIVISION OF HENRY HOLT AND COMPANY • NEW YORK

Twenty-First Century Books
A Division of Henry Holt and Company, Inc.
115 West 18th Street
New York, NY 10011

Henry Holt® and colophon are trademarks of
Henry Holt and Company, Inc.
Publishers since 1866

Published in Canada by Fitzhenry & Whiteside Ltd.
195 Allstate Parkway, Markham, Ontario, L3R 4T8

Library of Congress Cataloging-in-Publication Data
Seuling, Barbara.
To be a writer: a guide for young people who want to write and publish/
Barbara Seuling.
p. cm.
Includes bibliographical references and index.
Summary: Provides advice for those who want to become
writers, discussing such topics as telling a good story,
creating heroes and villains, and playing with words.
1. Authorship—Juvenile literature.
[1. Authorship 2. Creative writing.] I. Title
PN159.S48   1997   96-47653
808'.02—dc21   CIP
                                                    AC
ISBN 0-8050-4692-5
First Edition—1997

Designed by Kelly Soong

Printed in the United States of America
All first editions are printed on acid-free paper ∞.

1 3 5 7 9 10 8 6 4 2

This book is dedicated to
Jennifer Beth Antonelli

ACKNOWLEDGMENTS

My special thanks to Winnette Glasgow, for her endless patience in reading my many revisions and for her excellent insights;

to Pamela Seuling, whose early love for writing and continuing growth as a young writer inspired this book;

to Ginny Koeth, my editor, for her patience and belief in what I was doing as I roamed the cyberspace highways;

to Marvin Terban, my grammar mentor, who is always on call whenever I need help with some mind-twisting rule of the English language;

to Bonnie, Ellen, Fran, Marvin, Miriam, Peter, and Sandra—my writers' group—for their steadfast support and encouragement;

to Lindy Cady and Sue Hamen, for sharing their knowledge about special state events for young writers;

and to all the kids online and off who shared with me their opinions, writings, tips, advice, chats, newspapers, magazines, E-zines, and support during the writing of this book, especially Karen Zaino, Alexis Miseyko, Rachel Sipe, and Deborah Castellano, for sharing about clubs and publishing, and Kyle Cady, Jacob Walls, and Ian Sanford, for sharing their experiences at the 12th Oregon Writing Festival.

CONTENTS

1

"HELP! I NEED AN IDEA!"

Ideas are the foundation of all writing, whether it is poetry, stories, or books on how to build birdhouses. The challenge every writer faces is how to shape an idea into what she wants it to become.

Some people are lucky. Ideas come to them easily, like ripe fruit falling off a tree. Their notebooks burst with their ideas. Just give them a pencil and paper, and they're off. Others need help to bring ideas to mind—give them a title, for example, and they can write a story to go with it. Or suggest a topic, and they break loose into a writing marathon.

NO RIGHT OR WRONG WAY

There is no right or wrong way to begin. There are surely as many different ways to get started as there are different kinds of writers, and each writer has to find her own best path. You don't have to wait for inspiration to hit you like a brick falling from the sky if you're not one of those lucky ones just mentioned who come up with ideas easily. Try this:

- *Make a list called Situations. List interesting things that have happened to you. Maybe you misunderstood where to meet your mom at the mall one day and she reported you kidnapped. Maybe you baby-sat for a small terror who locked himself in the bathroom, or you discovered your best friend was a shoplifter.*

- *Make another list called Characters. List your aunt who talks to her plants, or a kid who trips over his pants because they're always too long, or a neighbor who owns a vicious dog.*

MIX AND MATCH

You might come up with ideas for articles about what to do if you're kidnapped, or tips for baby-sitters.

If you prefer writing stories, take one person and one situation and put them together for an interesting idea. Imagine your aunt shoplifting, or the kid with the long pants tripping over them as he runs from the vicious dog. When you put things together in a new or unusual way, story ideas just start to happen.

Your emotions when you come up with these ideas might lead you to write poetry, since poems spring from feelings. Finding out your friend is a shoplifter can leave you with some powerful feelings, for example.

Another way to generate ideas is to talk to other people and ask them to remember something interesting that once happened to them. Your grandparents probably have great stories to tell about what it was like when they were kids.

START WITH A PICTURE

Stories can start with a picture in your head of something happening to somebody. Get it clear. Maybe see it in motion, like a movie. Then write down what's happening in that picture.

Your thoughts and feelings about things that are going on in the world around you can help you come up with ideas. How do you feel about animal rights? Girls playing football? Vegetarianism? Having your own room?

KEEP A JOURNAL

Writing your thoughts in a diary or journal each day, or every few days, can help you recall experiences. You can go back to your entries later and see how you felt on an occasion, instead of trying to remember the exact emotions when you have forgotten some of the details. You can also see what was important to you at a certain stage in your life.

SHARE AN IDEA

If you know other young writers, it might be fun to come up with an idea for everyone to write about. (There's more about starting your own writing club or group on page 59.) No two writers will do the same thing with the same idea. Author Johanna Hurwitz provided strong evidence of this in a book of stories she compiled. She gave the same basic idea to several authors: *A birthday present arrives, beautifully wrapped, but there is nothing inside.* Each author turned that single idea into a completely different story. The book is called *Birthday Surprises . . .* check it out.

You never know when a good idea will fall into your lap.

They're all around you, everywhere, but you have to open your mind to them or they'll pass you right by. No matter how ordinary the setting appears to be—getting braces, a family argument over who gets to use the computer—any of these can be the source of a story idea. Familiar situations, or even dreams, make interesting reading for most people because they can imagine themselves in those situations.

ANOTHER POINT OF VIEW

If you're really stuck for an idea sometime, take a book you've read or a documentary you've seen and write a scene from another point of view. What about the story of *Jaws* from the shark's point of view, or an article showing why most sharks are not all that scary?

Sometimes your topic is chosen for you. A magazine contest may ask you to write on a theme—the environment, a humorous experience, or your favorite teacher. A school report may be connected to what you're studying, like medieval history.

ENDLESS CHOICES

When you have the freedom to choose your own topic, the range of choices is endless and sometimes that makes it difficult to know what to write about. A great way to choose a topic is to think about what you'd like to know, like who builds the best racing cars or how food gets to people in Antarctica, or how famous people got their first breaks.

Any idea that captures the imagination can get you started. Your curiosity to explore and investigate an idea carries it forward. Author James Cross Giblin once happened to sit next to a young chimney sweep on an airline flight, and they got to talking. Giblin's natural curiosity and his interest in history kicked in, and he ended up writing an award-winning book, *Chimney Sweeps*. Chances are, if you are fascinated by a particular idea, someone else will be too.

BRAINSTORMING

Do you see your writing as a short piece for a magazine, a poem, a nonfiction article, or as a book with chapters? Seeing your idea from various angles and imagining it in all possible forms is part of a process called *brainstorming*, which generally reveals the best way to shape your idea.

NARROW IT DOWN

If your topic is too big, you'll have too much information to cover. Whales, for example, is such a big subject (no pun intended) that you'd have to spend a lot of time on general information about all whales before you get into any details that we haven't heard before. If you narrow it down to one type of whale, like the blue or the humpback, you can be more specific about that whale's features, like how it gets its food, or its migration patterns, or fascinating statistics about it. Keep narrowing your topic down and see what you come up with: *whales—humpback whales—how humpback whales communicate—the songs of the humpback whales—recording the songs of the humpback whales for a commercial album.*

Let's say your idea is about a teenager who is lost on a hike in the mountains. That's pretty general. Kick that idea around. You may think of writing an article about an actual expedition in which there was a single survivor.

Ask "What if . . . ?" and see the possibilities that arise. *What if* nobody knows where this kid has gone? *What if* he was with a group, and they were all hurt or killed in some accident while he was off somewhere? *What if* he has a medical problem and must get help or he'll die?

As you bounce an idea around, each different turn means you have to make choices. You can toss out ideas or add them in—it's up to you. This brainstorming is leading you to a story.

TWENTY-FIVE WORDS OR LESS

When you think you know the story you want to tell, test your idea to see if it's ready. Sum up the plot in a simple sentence of twenty-five words or less. Introduce your main character and the story problem, and tell what the story is about. (It's not as easy as it sounds!)

> *Phil gets lost on a mountain hike.*

> *Phil gets lost on a mountain hike and has to find his way home.*

> *Phil, a diabetic, gets lost on a mountain hike and is running out of medicine.*

These ideas are not ready. They tell us who the main character is, Phil; but the first one doesn't give enough information, the second is a plot but isn't much of a story, and the third seems more like a story about a boy with diabetes than a boy surviving a hiking tragedy. Try it again.

> *Phil, the only survivor of a tragic hiking accident, has to get home before his medication runs out.*

That's better, with the emphasis on the hiking tragedy. The most important and interesting information is still there, the time pressure about the medication gives it tension, and it sounds interesting, with a real story line, or plot. With just eighteen words, it feels right.

Try another one, to get the feeling for it.

Joanna's dog, Vinnie, is lost.

Again, there's not enough information. This tells us who the main character is (Joanna) and the situation (losing her dog), but what is the plot or story plan?

Joanna's dog, Vinnie, is lost, and Joanna won't go home without him.

That's better. You can feel the difference. In the second version, we know what Joanna plans to do to change the situation. The first example has no tension, but the second example does, because we don't know what may happen when Joanna goes off to find Vinnie.

This one-sentence summary of your plot is a good test because it tells you if your story is ready to develop or if the idea is still too raw.

TIME TO MAKE A PLAN

Once your idea is ready, it's time to make a plan. Oops! you say . . . this sounds like outlining. Well, maybe it is, but I like to call it "story sketching" or "plotting." Whatever you call it, plotting works.

You'd probably like to overlook this part. After all, when you have an exciting new idea to carry you along, you have no trouble writing. You want to just plunge in. You can do that, of course, if it works for you. A lot of times, though, writers get stuck. They get a character in a situation and can't get him out again, or there's too much beginning and not enough middle, or the characters are confusing. A smart writer doesn't write first and try to fix it later. It's now, before the writing, during the brainstorming and plotting, that your brain should go into action—*before* you plunge in.

2

FOLLOW THE YELLOW BRICK ROAD

Most of us have to follow some map, or plan, that shows us how to get where we're going. Plotting is a fiction writer's road map.

Fiction is made up. Short stories and novels are fiction. So are TV dramas, plays, and movies. Shakespeare wrote fiction, even though he based some of it on historical fact. Stephen King and R. L. Stine write fiction, no matter how real they make it seem. Whenever you write a story, whether it's a mystery, science fiction, horror, or historical, it's fiction if you make it up.

THINKING IT THROUGH

When you write fiction, you create characters and put them into situations and settings. You tell them what to say and how to say it. Sounds easy, right? Only those who have tried to write stories know that it's not as easy as it sounds. Some writers get stuck and don't know how to move the story along. Some write stories that all come out the same. Others don't know how to end their stories. You can avoid these problems by thinking your story through in steps and anticipating problems before they develop.

An artist makes a rough sketch before she does a final drawing or painting. An architect has a blueprint. A director blocks out movements on a stage. Few artists go right for the final work without preliminary planning. The writer sketches too, but in words. The story sketch, or plot outline, shows you how to get where you're going.

In your sketch, you show what the story problem is, how it affects your character, and what he does to solve it. You spread the story out in steps, so you can see how it moves along. Your sketch can be as rough and tumble as you want it to be, or as organized as the outline method you learned in school, as long as it includes all the important parts and you can follow it.

Let's take that idea about the teenager lost in the mountains and give it another spin. We have the character and the situation—a teenage survivor of a tragic accident lost in the mountains—but let's make it happen in another time and place. Instead of a hike and an accident, we'll make it a wagon train that meets with tragedy. Let's test the idea.

Jeremiah, the only survivor of a wagon train disaster, must find his way across the mountains before the winter weather sets in.

SKETCHING IT OUT

Fine. Twenty-two words. This is the plot. The main character and the situation are stated clearly. Notice that the diabetes has been replaced by the threat of bad weather, which seemed more in keeping with the period. Here's how you might sketch out this story.

1. *Taking all the food he can carry with him, Jeremiah sets out to find the land his family was headed for. At night, exhausted, he sleeps in a cave. (This shows the main character and the situation, and has him starting out to solve the problem.)*

2. *The next day Jeremiah runs into bandits who steal his jacket and food, and leave him stranded. He survives by finding food and water and shelter. (This gets the story off to an exciting start, giving Jeremiah challenges to face. How he meets those challenges shows the reader what kind of person he is.)*

3. *Jeremiah stumbles upon a couple of trappers making a camp. They share water and food and advise him about a shorter route, one his father had refused to consider. (This helps the plot develop, introducing some mystery about Jeremiah's father.)*

4. *Jeremiah doesn't know why his father would not follow this route, but he takes it because it's shorter. Along the way, he learns why his father wanted to avoid it. (Figure out what this is later . . . maybe it reveals something important about his father or his background, or maybe it's just something practical, like it was too steep and craggy for the wagon.)*

5. *The path is narrow and uneven, and Jeremiah slips and falls down a steep ravine, hurting his leg. He wraps a torn piece of cloth from his shirt around the wound and continues on his way. (This increases the story tension and also shows his determination to survive.)*

6. *Jeremiah has learned to find food and shelter (the details of the story will show how he does this), but he is discouraged. He doesn't know if he'll make it. (This is a low point. Jeremiah feels that he will never see the land his father talked about.)*

7. *Just when everything looks hopeless, Jeremiah finds a small, weak animal shivering in a hollow by his cave. It's a baby. Jeremiah tries nursing it back to health. This takes his mind off his own problems for the moment. (This scene serves as a relief for the reader, who has been with Jeremiah through a grueling adventure. Perhaps the orphaned animal triggers Jeremiah's feelings about the loss of his own family.)*

8. *The animal survives. Jeremiah's strong attachment to it helps him over his own despair. When the little animal recovers, Jeremiah continues his journey with renewed confidence. (I'm getting close to the end now, so this has to pull my main character along toward the solution of the story problem. I haven't decided yet whether Jeremiah keeps the animal as a pet through the rest of his journey or if he lets it run free before he takes off again.)*

9. *After months in the wilds of the mountains, alone, scavenging for food and water, and finding warmth and shelter, Jeremiah reaches the place on the other side of the mountains he had heard his father speak about many times. (There will be something here showing that Jeremiah understands now what his father tried to tell him about this new land.)*

Now you have a plan, a map, a yellow brick road. You may not end up in Oz, but you have your story laid out so you can follow it and get where you want to go. This method doesn't do the writing for you, nor does it guarantee you won't have problems, but a story sketch sure makes writing easier.

You don't have to list every step along the way—you may not even know some of them yet. Show a clear beginning and ending, and the big steps in between to explain how your hero tries to solve the problem. Include a good amount of struggle along the way, because that will keep your reader interested in the character and the outcome.

You can make all the changes you want to at this point—the basic plan keeps the story on track. Even drastic changes, like changing the boy to a girl, or setting the story in the past rather than the present day, should not throw you. In Jeremiah's story, there were several changes and there may be others. The weather problem was introduced long after the outline was done. There are still many things to work out, but the basic story is set.

I'd still have to think about step 6. I don't know if Jeremiah's despair is enough of an obstacle, before everything begins to turn out all right. It's passive and quiet, rather than active. At this point in the story, I need a major conflict, with lots of action. Perhaps an attack by a bear or getting caught in an undertow as he's crossing a river would make a better story. I promised the reader a good adventure, and I want to fulfill that promise right up until the end. So this part may change to make it really tense and interesting.

Although there are still parts of the story to work out, at least it is written down. This story now has a good chance of making it.

You may not start out to write a book, but it can happen. This sketch is for a short story, but if there is enough "meat" in it, the story about Jeremiah could become a novel. In a short story, the number and depth of the adventures would have to be kept down to fit the size of a story but still give it tension and interest. A short story would need to move along faster and have much less description than a book. I'd show Jeremiah's thoughts and feelings through his actions.

In your plan, you can see how much time and space should be left for each step. Things should come out pretty well balanced, with none of the steps taking over the whole story. You know there has to be conflict throughout the story to keep the reader in suspense, but the problems can be varied: weather, animal danger, and robbers. It's good too to have both inner and outer conflict. For Jeremiah, struggling against physical obstacles is the outer conflict, while struggling to overcome his feelings of hopelessness is the inner conflict.

STAYING ON TRACK

You will find, if you write plays, that the outline is particularly good for keeping you on track. When you depend entirely on people speaking to each other, as you do in a play, the dialogue can lead you off on a line you didn't mean to take, or get you stuck in one place for too long. The outline reminds you that you have to move forward while you keep your characters talking.

Whether you like to write stories or plays, short stories or novels, fantasy or realistic stories, all the rules of good writing apply. The only things that will change are things specific to that particular type of writing.

In mystery stories, for example, planting clues is a standard part of plotting. Letting the solution come out bit by bit, or all at once at the end, is a big decision for you to make. It's important to maintain suspense throughout, and to give the reader enough clues to be able to figure out parts of the solution along with the hero as he reads, even though you have to be clever enough to keep the final solution a surprise until the end.

In writing a biography, your subject must be interesting to young people. Your job is to show the reader how the subject of your biography influenced the world we live in and why we are better off—or not—for it. You must portray the person's early life so the reader can see how different experiences might have affected her thoughts and behavior.

Fantasy and science fiction are popular types of fiction, and may take readers to places that are different from what they know. Often, what makes the experiences believable is that the characters start out in the real world. They are transported somehow to a place where customs and rules are different, and at the end are brought back to the real world. Examples of this kind of writing are found in Madeleine L'Engle's *A Wrinkle in Time* and C. S. Lewis's *The Lion, the Witch, and the Wardrobe*.

BEGIN WITH SOMETHING INTERESTING

If you know you are going to write a book, plan for each chapter to begin with some interesting action. Aim for two or three complete scenes in each chapter. Just as each chapter moves your story forward, each scene should move the chapter forward.

The same rules apply in writing a play, with each act or scene moving the story forward. Here, however, you must visualize movements and how characters will use the space onstage as the story unfolds, and you must create a setting in which all the dramatic action can be acted out, since the setting usually doesn't change much in the course of the play.

Now you are ready for your first draft, when you write your story for the first time. Keep a copy of the plot outline on your desk so you have a constant reminder of what your character is doing and where the story is going. Then write.

3

TELLING A GOOD STORY

Fiction is the art of telling a story—of making the reader believe
totally in the world and characters you create.

You've been telling stories all your life. When something happened at school, you came home and told your mom about it. You made up stories for your little sister at bedtime. When you saw a movie you liked, you told your friend about it. You knew how to hold the listener's attention; you sensed what would make her laugh, or want to hear more. You also knew how to make it sound weird, or scary, or magical.

MAKING IT MORE EXCITING

Your first draft is a lot like telling a story to a friend. You're not trying to make it perfect. You're looking for the best way to tell what you know, for the best possible reaction. You discover ways to make it sound more exciting. You don't stop to check spelling. Write from your gut as quickly as it comes, to capture the excitement you feel.

Once the first draft is written down, you can relax. Now you can think each part through more carefully. With your plot outline next to you, you can't go wrong.

Hook Your Reader

Read your opening line. It should "hook" the reader. Like the TV commercial that promises something wonderful about its product so that you can't wait to try it, your opening has to lure the reader into the story, so you promise something too—an interesting story. One method that works is to show your hero in action right away—in your very first sentence if you can.

Cal dodged the truck that came barreling down the street.

You can also hook your reader with dialogue, which is another kind of action. Dialogue brings a scene to life.

"Cal! Watch out!"
Cal jumped out of the way as a truck barreled past him.

Either of these openings promises something interesting ahead.

Tell Your Reader What to Expect

Shortly after your opening, give the reader some idea of what to expect without giving too much away. A good story is always about some problem, and about who has it and what he does about it. Hint at what that problem might be—or say it right out if you can do it—by the end of the first two or three paragraphs.

What you say and how you say it—the tone—will tell your reader what type of story it is—mystery, humor, historical, adventure, science-fiction, horror, etc.

Brian crept quietly around to the back of the house to look in the window. Just as he'd expected, the missing computer sat on the desk. He was right all along. Mr. Hendricks, the math teacher, was stealing the school's equipment.

There's no doubt this is going to be a mystery.

In another opening, we're caught up right away in the heroine's behavior.

Karen found herself wandering again. Whenever she thought about going home, and her father, her feet seemed to take her somewhere else.

You don't know much about the story—nothing has been revealed to spoil it for you—but it's clear that something disturbs Karen about her father, and you have the beginning of a dramatic story.

GIVE YOUR READER SOME BACKGROUND

Of course, you have to give your reader some necessary background information before too much time goes by—where the hero lives, how he gets along in school, who his friends are, and why he sometimes wears mismatched clothing. Providing these details—called exposition—is crucial to your reader's understanding of the character's thoughts and actions. Most of this information will come through in the early part of your story; just don't try to stuff it all into the opening or your reader will be bored to death before he's begun. Once you have his interest, provide just enough background for him to make sense of the hero's actions and appreciate how the hero got to this point and why he feels compelled to do something about the situation.

Conflict Is Necessary

The middle of your story should take the original problem and make it grow, and spread, in size and tension. This is the longest part, and you want your reader to be engrossed. As the story goes along, throw in some struggles, or conflict.

If Elizabeth wants a dog and gets it without any trouble, that's nice for Elizabeth, but it makes a boring story. If Elizabeth wants a dog and there's no way her family will let her have one, that brings conflict to your story and makes it more interesting; *how* interesting depends on what Elizabeth does about the situation. If she is determined to get a dog anyway, no matter what, she has an obstacle to overcome, and that creates tension, which is excellent for a story. You can't have things go too smoothly or the reader will just yawn. Make her worry!

Show, Don't Tell

Use action or dialogue to show what's happening in your story. In Scott O'Dell's *Sing Down the Moon*, the rebellious runaway slave, a Nez Perce girl, Nehana, knows the slave owners are on her trail. The author could have written:

Nehana felt desperate.

That would *tell* us what Nehana is feeling, but we would not see it for ourselves. Instead, he *shows* us, by using the character's own words to describe what she feels. Nehana says, "*I would rather die than be captured again.*" Hearing Nehana's own words is much more effective in bringing the situation to life and in getting the reader more emotionally involved.

Use description when you must, but use it with care. A little goes a long way. Try to get your reader to visualize the scene through the actions of your characters instead of using straight description. Following is a brief entry from the journal of Catherine in Karen Cushman's *Catherine, Called Birdy*.

I tried after dinner today to get George to play chess with me, but he said he promised the Lady Aelis a walk to acquaint her with our manor. Corpus bones! It is moat and muddy yard, house and stables and barn, dovecote, privy, and pig yard. She could see it all from the hall door.

Look at how the author has described Catherine's environment. Although you're getting information, you're caught up in Catherine's view of things and the actions of your characters, which is much more interesting than a flat description of the setting.

Toward the end of your story, but not quite, you have to take all that you've been building up to and reach a climax, or "black moment," where it looks as if everything is hopeless and nothing will work out right. Then, of course, there's some kind of turnaround and the day is saved. At least, that's the way it works for most stories. The reader is taken along on some kind of adventure or drama, reaches a peak, and then comes through it and ends the story in a satisfying way.

END YOUR STORY QUICKLY

When the problem you started out with is solved, there's no more story. End your story quickly. A few closing lines should do the trick.

As you think about these various points of fiction writing, you are absorbing ideas. These ideas will take shape in your writing as you practice more and more. It will take time before you master them all. Meanwhile, it's comforting to know that these techniques are now in your writer's bag of tricks.

HEROES AND VILLAINS

Some writers start a story with a situation. Others start with a character. Either way, you can't have one without adding the other pretty quickly.

Whatever the problem of the story is, it must affect your main character to the point where he has to do something about it.

Let's say there's a mean teacher in school. Your hero—the protagonist—tries to avoid this teacher, which is sometimes impossible. If your hero has to be at football practice at three o'clock on Tuesday, this teacher will find some way to keep him after school that day. If he doesn't practice, he'll be thrown off the team. How he overcomes or avoids this problem is pretty much what your story is about.

YOUR HERO HAS A JOB TO DO

Your hero definitely has a job to do—solving the plot problem. You want to show how smart or clever or strong he is, so you'll

31

use situations to show off these various attributes. Don't get carried away, though. Don't pile one adventure on top of another so that your hero begins to look superhuman. Make him believable for his age and circumstances.

Know Your Character Well

You can see how important it is to know your main character well—you have to know what's important to him and what he's capable of doing or saying. A character profile, or study, can help you determine these things.

Write a full page describing your main character as though you were giving a detailed report to someone who has to find him. Include anything you know about him, even silly things, like the kinds of things you know about your best friend—he can wiggle his ears, turns bright red when a girl speaks to him, and acts macho even though he's terrified of fighting. You may not use most of this information in your story, but now you can picture your hero moving through the story more clearly. Your knowledge of your character will come across as you make him more convincing to the reader through an attitude, a phrase, or an action.

In L. Frank Baum's *The Wizard of Oz*, no matter how strange or frightening her experiences, Dorothy is always the well-brought-up farm girl who is kind and courteous to everyone, even to the wicked witch. It would be surprising to suddenly have her do something out of character or think of herself before her friends.

Write character profiles for secondary characters as well—those who have medium-size roles in your story. They have a part to play too. They support your main character in what he's trying to accomplish and show us things about the hero as they interact with him. Different characters will notice different things—a sense of humor, a quick temper, or a stubborn streak.

USE CONTRASTS

A character who spends a lot of time with the main character, like a best friend, should be a contrast to the main character in some important way, to keep the two characters from being confused with each other. This contrast can be in personality, physical appearance, or both. If your main character is serious and logical, his best friend might be funny and impulsive.

Anyone who tries to prevent the hero from reaching his goal, like the Joker in the Batman stories, is the antagonist. The antagonist can be nonhuman, like the frozen tundra in Jean Craighead George's *Julie of the Wolves*.

CHOOSE THE VIEWPOINT THAT FEELS RIGHT

A story is almost always told from the main character's viewpoint. That means seeing the world as that character sees it. If your story is told from the point of view of an old man, you have to see the world as that old man sees it. If your story is told from the viewpoint of a pig, get into the mind of the pig to see the world as a pig sees it. It wouldn't be too crazy to get down on all fours to get a real feeling for the pig's view of things! Don't mix several viewpoints in the same story. It will bounce your reader around like a rubber ball.

Another thing to think about is whether to write your story in the first person or the third person. First person means writing in the voice of the character as though she is doing the writing. In this example from *The Cat Ate My Gymsuit*, author Paula Danziger writes from the viewpoint of the protagonist, Marcy Lewis:

We figured that Ms. Finney must be sick or taking a mental-health day to recuperate from teaching us.

If you don't want to be limited to speaking exactly as the main character speaks, write in the third person. That's the "he," "she," "they" viewpoint. This scene from *Trouble Will Find You* by Joan Lexau is about Desmond (Diz) Aster, and it's told from his point of view, but it's told in the third person by a narrator.

"We'll just explain to the police," Diz said. "Then it will be over."
"I hope so," Pepper said.
Diz hoped so, too.

The first person is much more personal. The third person makes you feel as if you're standing back a little so you can see everything more clearly. Try them both and choose the viewpoint that feels right for your story.

AN INVISIBLE GUIDE

No matter which viewpoint you choose, there is always a narrator, the one who is telling the story. The narrator is like an invisible guide, pulling the reader along, observing what's going on, and deciding what happens next. Sometimes the narrator is a character in the story and it's pretty obvious who it is. Other times it's a separate voice, like someone looking in on the scene from an outside position, detached from the story yet able to see and hear all.

Your hero should not solve the story problem quickly. If he succeeds right away, the story is over. A setback or two before he succeeds keeps the reader guessing. Usually, the hero succeeds eventually, in spite of the odds. Your story doesn't have to have a happy ending, but most stories end up at least on a positive note.

Dialogue is excellent for brightening up a page and bringing a scene to life. It can also be used to help distinguish one character from another and to tell something about those characters, as in this bit from Richard Peck's *The Ghost Belonged to Me*:

> *"Hello, Brother dear," Lucille said to me and whipped up all the hair on my head as she slid her sizable bottom into a chair.*
> *"Lemme alone," I greeted her.*

Just look at what you know from this tiny snatch of dialogue: the boy's sister is hefty, and a tease, and he is not amused by her.

As a writer, always be on the alert for how people in real life speak to each other so you can learn what you have to capture in your writing. It's especially important to write dialogue that sounds natural if you write plays, which are entirely in dialogue. Dialogue is tricky, because you don't want to resort to shortcut language like "gonna" for "going to," yet you want people to sound natural. Your ear will begin to pick up the sounds and phrases that work to make the transfer of dialogue from life to print acceptable, and even invisible.

SPEND TIME WITH YOUR CHARACTERS

When you remember a story, it's probably the strong characters you recall, like Captain Ahab in Herman Melville's *Moby Dick* and Heathcliff in Emily Brontë's *Wuthering Heights*. When you create characters, spend plenty of time with them. Get to know them. Give them unique personality traits that they can use in your story. Then your characters will be memorable too.

5

NOTHING BUT
THE TRUTH

Good nonfiction writing is just as interesting and lively as good fiction; the reader doesn't want to put it down.

Nonfiction is factual. You read it every day in biographies, dictionaries, newspapers, driver's manuals, articles about space shuttles or the latest comings and goings of pop music stars. A lot more space in magazines is devoted to nonfiction than fiction. Even folktales and poetry are classified as nonfiction.

You may have had a brush with the kind of nonfiction writing known as journalism if you worked on a school newspaper, covering news and reporting on current issues. Other nonfiction writing you know is the essays and reports you have done for school assignments.

GETTING IT OFF YOUR CHEST

An essay expresses your feelings about something. You don't have to convince anyone else with an essay—it just gets something off your chest. Maybe you want to say what you think about a certain rock band being banned from a park in your area, or how you believe vegetarianism can save the planet.

Exploring in Depth

A report explores a topic in depth. It is researched, organized, and presented to inform the reader. If there is some controversy about the subject, both sides are shown. Reports are generally organized into three sections—the introduction of the topic, the body (like the meat in the sandwich), and the conclusion. Reports for school are designed to teach you how to research and organize your thoughts.

Articles are similar to reports in many ways, but they are written for the public. Readers pay for the magazines they read, and expect not only carefully researched information but lively and entertaining writing at the same time.

Poetry Is About Feelings

Poetry is an expression of feelings that you want to hold on to in words. It can be short, as in haiku, or go on for pages. It can be about anything. As in all writing, it comes from your own experiences, mixed with ideas that you borrow from outside yourself. As the author, you can decide whether your poem will be funny, or serious, or scary. Although poetry is classified as nonfiction, it is often about situations you have never experienced before, and you use your imagination to guide you.

Like a Tour Guide

An outline—even a very rough one—can help you keep your material organized. Just as in fiction, the outline is a guide to help you remember to balance out your information and to cover certain points. It's particularly helpful in nonfiction, where some of your research can get you into pretty interesting areas—and take you way off the track.

Make the Reader Want to Know More

Open your article with something that appeals to the reader right away. Remember the "hook" you learned about for fiction? Use it here too. You must catch the reader's attention with a bit of information or action that promises something interesting will follow.

> *Out in the Gulf of Maine, a whaling ship cruises quietly. A splash off the port side spurs the crew to action. They reach for cameras, instruments and charts. This crew has been waiting for the humpback whales to return.*

You can see that this sets the tone, and tells the reader what this article is about. It also makes the reader want to know more. Think in terms of a question your article will answer.

- *How do the scientists know these are the same whales year after year?* or

- *How has this kind of study helped the humpback whale?*

Jump Right In

Another way to begin is to jump right in with a topic sentence, one that tells exactly what you're going to talk about in this article. *The humpback whales were back again and the marine scientists were there, waiting for them.*

The body of an article, or the middle, carries out the idea

presented in the opening and supplies information in detail that supports the main idea. You might offer interesting statistics, quote from an interview with a marine biologist, or give examples of actual whale-watching voyages to bring the material to life. You can borrow a trick from news reporters, who are trained to answer the 5 Ws: Who? What? Where? When? Why? In this section, present your information, leading up to the conclusion—the answer to the question(s) your article has raised.

The ending summarizes the information, and reminds the reader of the point of the article. Your conclusion should bring your report to a satisfactory end. Perhaps you'll want to bring your readers back to your opening idea, showing how this study of the humpback whales in the Gulf of Maine contributes to our knowledge of the humpback whale or helps to protect them from extinction.

Poking Around

Before you get involved in a topic, do a little preliminary research to get some feeling for the subject. An encyclopedia entry or an article in a magazine can get you started. How much research you do later will depend on how much time you have and how long the report will be. This preliminary poking around saves lots of time. You may find out that even though your idea seems terrific, there is not much information available about it for your article, or there may be so much information to sort out, it will take too long to do the job properly in the time you have.

Once you are sure about your topic, you will need to learn more about it—enough to understand it thoroughly and present it to your readers intelligently. We'll talk more about this kind of research in the next chapter.

The best article or report gives the reader a general understanding of your subject, as well as solid, specific information about it. Select the facts you feel are necessary to do this, and write about them clearly, explaining important points as you go.

You Can Write a Book

If you have plenty to say, and want lots of room to say it, you can choose to write a book. Nonfiction books range from photo–essay picture books to older and more sophisticated books, with a lot of other examples in between, like books on how to make model airplanes or understanding what makes earthquakes happen.

If you choose to write a book, your research will take you a lot longer than research for an article, because there is so much more ground to cover. Start with the background to your topic and why you are writing this book. Divide the subject into sections, or chapters. Later, you will gather all the information you can for each chapter and then summarize what each chapter is about. There should be a flow of material that keeps expanding and enlarging on the basic theme as you go on.

A Title Should Give a Clue

Your title should give the reader a clue about the contents of your report. You wouldn't call your work "The Story of Dr. Edward Jenner" unless it is a complete biography of the man. If your article is on one of Dr. Jenner's experiments in an attempt to find a cure for smallpox, then the title should indicate that the article is *about* Dr. Jenner but deals with just one important episode in his life. "Dr. Jenner's Bright Idea" might be better, because it indicates that while Jenner is important, the article is about just one particular idea in his life.

When you are researching a nonfiction topic, your sources

should be the most current available. If you're writing about volcanoes, include the latest one of any significance as well as the most powerful one in history. List the sources you have used—books, articles, TV documentaries, videotapes, CD-ROM disks, and online services—to show the reader where you got your information and where she might go to find out more about the topic on her own. If you get information from the Internet, or any online service, be sure to copy down the source of the information you need. Anyone interviewed for your research should be listed, too, showing the name of the person interviewed, the person's connection to your subject, where the interview took place, and the date of the interview.

Computers and TV have improved the writer's ability to explore the world every day without having to leave home. Electronic tools and programs help you come up with ideas and show you how to organize them. CD-ROM gives you the ability to add pictures and sound to a report. Animation, movies, photographs, maps, art, and background sounds of people, places, and music can all be included in a project.

In a report on bridges you can show films of one bridge being built and another being destroyed, you can take your readers on a ride across the Brooklyn Bridge, show a photo of its architect, and play a recording of Simon and Garfunkel's "59th Street Bridge Song" all in one presentation. Writing about subjects that interest you can be as exciting to you as creating a story is for another writer. For some people, nonfiction is the only kind of writing.

GIVE CREDIT WHERE IT'S DUE

In your research you will find important information from people who have researched the same subject before you. You will want to use that information in your report or book. Some of this information will be found in encyclopedias and other reference books, but you may also find some in films, interviews, exhibits on your subject, online, or in other places. Just locating information is not the end of your work. No matter where you find your information, or how old it is, you must give credit to the original source.

You cannot copy someone else's words and pass them off as your own writing. This is called plagiarism and is the same as stealing someone's property. It's okay to quote a line or two exactly as the author wrote it if you tell the reader who the author is that you're quoting and where the quotation came from. When you want to use a great deal of the information you have found, tell the reader what you have learned about your subject in your own way, using your own words, and cite the sources for what you have learned in a bibliography at the end of your work.

STICK TO THE FACTS

Using the information you have collected, and following your outline, write your first draft. Just as you do in fiction, you can create a mood or establish a setting, but be careful not to invent dialogue or situations that never happened. Stick to the facts, and what is found and supported in public documents, journals, or quotations.

You can offer the reader the same drama, suspense, humor, surprise, and excitement as she finds in a good work of fiction. With nonfiction, you don't even have to make it up; it's all there, waiting for you to assemble it and present it to the reader.

6

ONE THING LEADS TO ANOTHER

The secret to good nonfiction writing is good research. Know your subject thoroughly, even if you use only a fraction of what you learn in your writing.

Never before has it been so exciting to do research. Libraries bulge with books and databases, TV and movies provide fascinating biographies and documentaries, and people are more inclined than ever to be interviewed for their opinions and expertise on certain subjects because exposure in all media is good for their public image. We also now have the Internet—a truly amazing research tool.

CRUISING THE INFORMATION HIGHWAY

If you have a computer and a modem and subscribe to one of the online services like *Prodigy* or *America OnLine*, you are probably familiar with the Internet, or the information superhighway. It's a vast system of computers—millions of them—

linked together in various networks around the world. By the time you graduate from high school, you and most of your friends will be cruising the Internet's highways and byways with speed and ease. You may even be doing it already.

The Internet originated with the U.S. Defense Department, supported by leftover funding from the space program. It soon spread to the medical profession, scientists, and educators, and is now accessible to anyone who can hook up to it electronically.

The World Wide Web (WWW) is a network of locations on the Internet. It's possible to browse through these using a software program generally supplied by your service provider. This "browser" helps you find what you're looking for.

SEARCHING FOR WEREWOLVES

What if you want to write an article about werewolves? You can look in the library, starting with the encyclopedia, which has a brief entry on werewolves. Jot down some notes, then try the card catalog or the database if your library has one. Both will show you what the library has available under the subject heading "werewolves." If you do not know how to use a database, ask the librarian for help. Don't forget to cross-reference—look up other categories where you may find information about werewolves. "Myths" and "folklore" might lead you to information about werewolves, or to information about "vampires," which are often associated with werewolves, so look them up as well.

Let's say you find four books listed—one scholarly tome written a century ago, two novels, and a nonfiction book, *Werewolves*, by Nancy Garden, published in 1973. The fiction might be fun but probably won't give you much concrete information. That ancient book sounds too heavy and old for your report. The Garden book is not exactly new, but it sounds good otherwise, and the publication date may not matter so much with this subject.

As you read the Garden book, you learn a lot about werewolves. A man in Germany in the 1500s went around killing people and eating them. The people of his town hunted him down and killed him, believing he was a werewolf. American Indians believed in some sort of shape-shifting, too. The author lists other books that she found helpful when she was doing her research. If you can find them, look them up. Read as much background material as you can, so you don't rely on just one author's view for your information.

Go to the Experts

Contact specialists and organizations who know about your subject. If you are interested in the latest findings regarding Jupiter or the Hubble Space Telescope, you would go to NASA, because they sponsor space projects. For an article about iguanas, you would contact a natural history museum or a local herpetological (reptile) society. Write, phone, fax, or use the Internet to contact the experts, but be prepared. Have a specific question ready. Don't ask someone to tell you all about something, like butterflies—that's too big a subject.

Primary sources are people, places, or things that were part of the original experience of an event you may be researching. Anne Frank is a primary source on the Holocaust . . . she lived during that time and wrote about it in her diary. The apartment in which she and her family hid, and the pictures of film stars that were pasted on her wall, are also primary sources. Autobiographies, bills of sale, letters, actual clothing worn by the subject, birth certificates, and recordings are also examples of primary sources. If you use material from any written primary sources, use quotation marks around anything you quote directly.

Interviews are excellent source material for writers. People are generally agreeable and willing to let you interview them or ask a few questions over the phone or by letter, as long as you aren't prying into personal matters. Set up interviews with people who have information on your subject. If you are doing a study of events that changed people's lives in the twentieth century, your grandmother or great-grandmother could be a primary source. She can tell you how World War II or the coming of TV changed her life when she was a girl, because she witnessed both events. The secret to a good interview is having lots of questions prepared ahead of time. A tape recorder is useful in an interview because you can go back over the material later, when you're doing your writing. Keep a notebook handy even if you use a tape recorder. It's good for taking down the exact spellings of names and places.

If you have access to the Internet, try a search for your subject. You have to do a little surfing, or exploring, with a software tool known as a "search engine" to find the best paths to your topic. Take "werewolves" again. The results of your search might list twenty different items mentioning werewolves. One of those might be for a rock band called "Werewolf." Another could be a horror film about werewolves. Keep looking until you find listings that sound right for you. One called "Society and Culture—Folklore" sounds good. Don't forget to cross-reference here too, checking topics that relate to your main subject. And don't forget to write down your sources, listing the name of the person or organization responsible for providing the information. Later, when you write up your report on werewolves in your own words, you will be able to cite those sources without confusion or needing to go back over some of your research a second time.

TAKE NOTES

As you research your subject, take notes—a word here, a phrase there—whatever helps you remember key points. Each time you finish with a source, write down two or three points that you got from it and a couple of questions that you would still like to have answered as you continue your research.

It's hard to know when to stop researching and start writing. You can divide your time equally among research, organizing your material, and writing, or maybe you'll want to spend more time on the research than on the writing. Your plan should suit your style and the time you have available to work on the project.

ONE SOURCE IS NOT ENOUGH

Collect plenty of information. One source is not enough—you need to support and confirm your facts, unless your source is well known and trustworthy, like the Smithsonian Institution. List carefully the exact information about the sources you use: the author (or authors) and title of the work, the publisher, and the date of publication. Not only will this help you in preparing your bibliography, but it will be useful if you have to return to any of your sources later on for any reason.

The neat thing about research is that it can be as much fun as the writing. If you find yourself losing track of time when you're doing research, better get yourself a watch with an alarm on it, because otherwise someone may find you in a dusty corner of some library, under a pile of notes, books, and papers, or out in cyberspace cruising the electronic highway!

7

PLAYING WITH WORDS

To be a writer is to be in charge of words, knowing what you want to say and how to say it, setting minds to thinking and hearts to racing.

You understood the power of words when you first learned to read. Reading let you enter magical worlds and go on exciting adventures. Since that time, you have cried over sad stories, laughed over funny ones, and read books that made you think harder than you have ever thought before. You met characters and got into situations far from your real, safe world. Now you are a writer, creating the words that will do this for other readers. Awesome. Better be sure the words you use are the very best.

DIG DEEPER

The English language is the richest language in the world. You don't have to use the first words that come to mind. There are better ones lurking beneath the surface. Dig a little deeper for more precise words. Use a thesaurus to help you mine for word gems. A dictionary tells what a word means, but the thesaurus lists a variety of other words that may be used in place of the one you chose.

If your heroine is in a big hurry, you might say she's "running" down the street, but that does not quite describe the action you have in mind. Check the thesaurus. Thirty verbs are listed for the word *run*. One of them is *sprint*, which is closer to the meaning you had in mind. Subentries under *sprint* give you several more choices—*race, dash, tear*. . . . That's it! *Tear.* "She tore down the street" is so much better than "She ran down the street." This one word seems to make a radical difference.

The wrong choice of words can make a perfectly good piece of writing dull. Action words pep up your writing. Go over the verbs you've used and see if they can be livelier.

A songwriter looking for lyrics knows how important word choices are. Look at the lyrics of one of your favorite songs and try to imagine why the writer chose those particular words.

TRICKS OF THE LANGUAGE

Studying poetry or the lyrics of songs can show you how authors use certain "tricks" of the language to get their ideas or images across. Shakespeare said, "My love is like a red, red rose," comparing his sweetheart to a beautiful flower. In the nursery rhyme about Mary and her little lamb, the author says the lamb's fleece was "white as snow." This kind of comparison is called *simile*. It shows that one thing is like another thing.

Another kind of language "trick" is metaphor, where you don't say one thing is *like* another; you say it *is* the other, giving an even stronger image to the reader. In metaphor, you would say your love *is* a flower, not like a flower. We often see people as animal-like, and use metaphor in such cases, as in "The old barracuda, Mrs. Dowd, addressed the meeting." Actions too can be described in metaphor, as in "He bulldozed his way across the forty-yard line."

You have probably read flowery description that doesn't add meaning to a story. Simile and metaphor can get images across quickly and punch up your writing without adding clutter.

She walked slowly through the cool, dark, shadowy woods as the icy late-autumn wind blew through the crisp yellow and orange leaves, causing some of them to fall, thickly covering the mossy ground.

Look what happens when you remove the clutter:

As she walked in the woods, yellowy orange leaves fluttered to the ground like butterflies, covering it in a thick blanket.

Note the omissions. Woods are generally sort of dark and shadowy. We know it's autumn by the colors and the falling leaves. It's not really important to say it's windy or cool . . . autumn is generally cool and breezy, and the leaves are blowing off the trees. Comparing the leaves to butterflies tells the reader not only that the leaves were falling but how they looked when they fell. Putting this kind of care into the words you choose takes more effort, but the images that result are much more satisfying.

USE ALL YOUR SENSES

Providing sensory detail—using the various senses of sight, hearing, touch, smell, and taste—is another way to give the reader vivid pictures of what you have in mind.

NOT JUST A GAME

Wordplay may be fun, but it's not just a game. It keeps language exciting and interesting. Authors use wordplay to name their characters or create titles. In *The Wolves of Willoughby Chase*, Joan Aiken has two little girls left in the care of a mean guardian, Miss Slighcarp. That's a wonderful name for a villain, and it gives the reader a sense of what to expect from that character. Other authors use the playful repetition of sounds that are close together—as in the *Amelia Bedelia* books, featuring Peggy Parrish's famous character, or *The Teeny Tiny Woman*, a story I adapted for a picture book.

Using two names in a story that begin with the same letter or sound (Jody and Jenny; Fred and Phil) or that sound alike (Jerry and Larry) can confuse the reader. On the other hand, you can reverse this idea to create a humorous situation. The popular cartoon characters *Huey, Dewey,* and *Louie* are three little ducks, but they behave as though they are one. Therefore, their names *should* sound alike.

CREATE IMAGES

Some sounds help to create images for the reader, like the train going *clackety-clack* down the track, or the lamb bleating for its mother, *baa baaa, baaaaaa*. Sounds can also make words seem tougher—*pitch, rasp, crank*—or softer—*smooth, lullaby*. Listen to something familiar—your pencil as you write, the plumbing when you flush the toilet, the wheels of your skates on the pavement—and try to capture that sound in writing.

Words may be chosen for their rhyme or rhythm as they are put together. This is obvious in some poetry, but it can be done with prose as well. Some words are chosen because they sound pretty, or funny, or weird. Lewis Carroll made up his own words for his poem "Jabberwocky," probably because they sounded just right to his ear and added to the humorous effect:

'Twas brillig, and the slithy toves
Did gyre and gimble in the wabe . . .

Your story or article may be packed with fascinating information, but a relentless drumming of words in the same patterns can put the reader to sleep. You need variety in your sentences. Look at the following paragraph:

> *Sam knocked at the cabin door. A bearded man opened the door and let him in. The man asked Sam to sit down. Sam sat in a chair by the table. He looked around the cabin. He saw a picture in a small gold frame. It was a photograph of a woman.*

A more interesting construction might be:

> *Sam knocked. A bearded man opened the cabin door.*
> *"Come in," he said.*
> *Sam entered the small cabin.*
> *"Please . . . have a seat," said the man, pulling a chair out.*
> *Sam sat down, looking around. His eyes rested on a small gold frame with a portrait of a woman in it.*

AIM FOR SIMPLICITY

The other extreme, constructing sentences that are so complex they boggle the mind, is just as bad. Richness of language doesn't mean making it more complicated. Your first obligation is to communicate, so aim for simplicity.

Think of images when you write. Try to *show* your reader what you see, hear, and feel. When another person reads your work, you want it to be as clear and as vivid as it was to you when you first wrote those words.

8

ONE MORE TIME!

Revision is to writing what polishing is to a jeweler—it brings out the luster of the raw gem.

First you write. Then you revise, and revise, and revise.

It's like preparing to meet someone important for the first time. You try on lots of clothes, and make lots of changes until you feel you look just right. Revising your writing is the same thing. You make changes until it comes out just right.

SEEING AGAIN

Revision is a natural part of writing. There are times when your writing comes out fine the first time around, but it doesn't happen often, even for professional writers. It's not unusual to go through three, twelve, twenty, even thirty revisions before a manuscript is ready. The number of times you revise has nothing to do with your ability—revision means "seeing again," perhaps noticing something you didn't see before.

You can start by editing yourself, checking first for content. If you have made changes from your original plan, be sure what you've written is the work you wanted it to be when you started out. If it's a story, does your main character solve the problem? Do you have a single viewpoint? Are the actions clear? Have you included any characters you don't really need? If your work is nonfiction, is your writing lively and is your information organized in an interesting way? Have you explained it clearly? Do you have a good opening? Did you sum things up neatly at the end?

Edit for language too. Exchange weak words for stronger ones. If the story drags suddenly, pep up the pacing with action words and shorter, sharper sentences. Look at your sentences for variety in length and style. Find places where your writing can be smoother, or more interesting. Choose the exact word you want instead of the first one that comes to mind. Has your language moved the reader? Is it delightful to the ear? Does it surprise and sway and ripple and pounce to give the reader clear and concrete images? Have you used sounds and smells and tastes to which the reader can respond?

Edit for length. Weed out unnecessary words. Avoid description that isn't absolutely necessary. A finished piece of writing (unless you're writing poetry) can almost always be reduced by at least 10 percent. This is not necessarily because there are too many words, but because there are too many words *for what you have to say.* Can you write the same sentence in fewer words? Are there tag lines ("he said," "she said") that can be removed without confusing the reader about who is speaking?

Get a Writing Buddy

What else can you do to help the reader find your work as funny, suspenseful, or fascinating as you meant it to be?

Sometimes it takes an outside reader to see how to improve a point.

After you've done your self-editing, call on a writing buddy, or a writing group if you have one. If there is no writers' club or group around, start one. Find other young people who like to write. A writing club can be two people who share their work and talk about writing, or it can be a school-sponsored club that ends up publishing a literary magazine of the members' work. It could be a group that meets in your room once a week, or an online club, where you meet with people on a screen instead of in person and you send each other work by e-mail. Sharing your work with others who also write and understand the problems of writing is great support for a writer.

In a writing group, you read your work to each other and critique it, or discuss its good points and where it can be improved. As you listen to work being read, jot down notes to help you remember what you want to say. When it's your turn to speak, start off with what you like about the work. Try to understand what the author tried to accomplish. Then explain why it did or didn't work for you. It's fine to offer suggestions, but be sure not to tell the writer what to write. From your reaction and suggestions, the author should have the freedom to work it out on her own.

When it's your turn to read, others will listen and give you their reactions to your writing. It's important to realize this is not an attack. Even if specific suggestions are made about how to improve your work, don't be defensive. Take notes instead. Later, when you are by yourself, weigh and consider the criticism. Keep your mind open to all possibilities. If you decide not to take a suggestion, that's okay; you're the boss. In the end, consider what can make your story or article stronger.

Let's look at what happens in a critique session. Someone

might comment: *"The beginning is slow. The story doesn't start quickly enough."*

The author considers this comment, and it helps her to see the problem. The main character should be doing something interesting in the opening scene. The author rewrites the scene.

She has her character doing something. Maybe she shows the heroine jumping up because a spider crosses her path, showing her fear of crawly things. This not only starts off with an interesting action; it also foreshadows a later scene in the story in which the heroine has to overcome that fear when she has to confront a snake.

POSSIBILITIES FOR IMPROVEMENT

In the revision stage, as you make one change something else may occur to you to make the story more interesting. This time around, with the help of self-editing as well as the feedback of other writers, you can see possibilities for improvement more clearly.

Read your revised work to the group again. This will show you whether or not you understood the advice you were given. If you have used it well and improved the areas that were unclear or weak, you have taken your work a step farther. A good writers' group will support and encourage you until your work has been brought to the highest possible level.

YOU DON'T HAVE TO LIKE IT

Nobody says you have to like revising your work. You'd just as soon have it come out perfectly the first time and go on to something else. Who wouldn't? But that's not realistic. Besides, you learn a lot when you get a chance to "resee" something.

Each time you make a change and see your writing come out better, you learn just what it took to make the improvement. Even if you don't like revising, you can appreciate it as part of the learning process and maybe that will help you live with it.

LIKE GROWING A PLANT

Revising your work is a little like growing a plant. You have to prune it and cut it back sometimes for it to grow properly. It takes time, but with proper care your plant finally blooms. When you revise, you are getting your work to blossom with a better choice of words, clever dialogue, a richer background, and more interesting characters. In general, your story becomes stronger, livelier, and more enjoyable.

9

FAME, FORTUNE, AND FREE COPIES

Although it isn't the only reason for writing, publishing your work and sharing it with others is pretty exciting.

The writing may be fun, the research may be interesting, and you think your work is pretty good. Then it comes to getting your work published and—*duh!*—your brain turns to oatmeal.

No Reason to Walk into Walls

There's no reason to feel you've walked into a wall at this point. Finding ways to publish your work is not as hard as it seems. You just have to know your way around.

Publishing means making your writing public. Printing multiple copies of your work and sharing it with others is publishing, even if it only puts your work into the hands of a few people.

There are many reasons why you might want to publish your own work. You can give a book of your poems to a friend. You can assemble a "Family History" with personal stories and remembrances of all the members of your family to give out at a family reunion. Your humorous sketches about the members of your team might be fun to share with them.

Your writing club may publish a newsletter or magazine, in which the work of members, including yours, is published. This doesn't take much more than a typewriter or computer, some paste or glue, a copying machine and some staples. If each member contributes to the cost, it shouldn't be difficult to manage. You might even print extra copies to give as gifts or sell to raise money for your club.

TRY THE SCHOOL NEWSPAPER

School is a great place to get your writing published. Creative writing is a regular part of studies in most schools, and class magazines and school newspapers are encouraged. You may even have the help of some snappy software products to help you organize, design, and print your work on the computer.

If your school has a newspaper, join the staff. Volunteer to be a reporter and cover school or community issues or do feature articles. If you have a specialty, like sports, the editor may agree to give you a regular column in the paper. A school paper or magazine is a good place for a writer to learn editorial skills.

If your school does not have either a newspaper or a literary magazine, get some interested writers together and petition your teacher or your principal to let you start one.

Give your newspaper or magazine a zippy name to reflect your style, and enlist the help of writers to report the news, and to turn in essays and stories, puzzles and reviews. Other students can join you on the staff to help collect articles by the deadline, to edit, and to lay out the paper. Get the magazine or newspaper out on a regular basis—once a month, perhaps—

and distribute it around the school and into the community. Get neighborhood businesses to take ads for a few dollars, and use the money to buy printing supplies.

Publishing Online

If your school has a computer setup with a modem, and you can get on the Internet, publish your newspaper online and distribute it to young people in other parts of the world. Invite kids in other countries to submit their news items and articles to your newspaper.

Publishing your work outside school or your community is much more difficult because there are many more professional writers to compete with. Knowing the markets, or publishers, that are available to you can help you get your work published. There is a listing of publishers and several market guides in the appendix to help you explore the markets for your writing in depth.

Many magazine and book publishers publish the work of writers up to the age of eighteen or nineteen. Most of them have guidelines—rules that must be followed when submitting work—that they will provide for free if you send them a self-addressed stamped envelope (a SASE) with your request.

Study the Magazines

Study an issue of the magazine to which you want to submit your work. This can help you decide if your work is really right for that publication. Does this magazine publish fiction or only articles? Will your subject matter appeal to readers of this magazine? Sending your work to the wrong market costs a lot of time and postage, not to mention hurt feelings when you get it back.

On the Internet, search under WRITING/KIDS for various

web sites that will link you to clubs for young writers, newspapers, and online magazines (called "E-zines") that publish the work of young writers, and other information that is entertaining and useful. Something to be aware of if you send work electronically is the need to add a copyright notice at the beginning of your work, such as *Copyright 5/18/(year) by Lotta Werdz*.

PROTECT YOUR WORK

Protecting your work is an important issue whether online or off. Keep a copy of everything you send out in print or electronically, with the date of copyright—the date you wrote it—on it. While this does not guarantee that your work will not be copied or stolen, the notice lets others know that you are the true owner of the work. When you belong to an online writers' club and you want to share your work with other club members, do it via e-mail rather than in a more public area; it's safer. The electronic highway is relatively new, and some of the kinks are still being worked out; when in doubt, and if you cherish a piece of work, send it to others you trust by regular "snail" mail.

It is not necessary to file your manuscript with the Register of Copyrights at the Library of Congress in Washington, D.C. The 1978 Copyright Act protects your work from the time it is first written to the length of your life plus fifty years. After a work is published, the publisher will copyright your manuscript as a published work.

There are dozens of contests (see Appendix B for a listing) to encourage young writers to send in their work. There are even book publishers that offer contracts as prizes to young writers. All contests have official rules and guidelines and offer specific rewards for winning, from free copies of the magazine to publication, money, and contracts. Most of these contests have entry forms that list the rules, which you must follow strictly. Remember to enclose a SASE whenever you write for information or entry forms.

Your manuscript should look like the sample pages on pages 97–98. As you type up your final draft, check the dictionary for spelling (or use the spell-check feature on your computer) and correct your punctuation and grammar. The publisher's guidelines will tell you if handwritten work is acceptable, but with computers available at libraries, schools, and friends' houses, try to type your work or have it printed out. A #10 business envelope will hold three to four pages, depending on the thickness of the paper, folded in thirds. Use a five-by-seven-inch envelope for five to ten pages, folded in half, and a nine-by-twelve-inch envelope for larger manuscripts. Always enclose a SASE with your manuscript so the publisher can reply to you and return your manuscript.

They Really Mean It

When a magazine states that stories can be up to eight hundred or a thousand words, they really mean it. You can go over a tiny bit—up to 10 percent more—but that's it. Anything longer than that will probably not be considered. Cut it down to size before you send it, or find a publisher who will accept longer stories.

The subject matter should appeal to the audience that reads the publication you're submitting your work to. If the publication is for adults, readers will want to read about other adults. If it's for a teenage audience, readers will want material that's interesting to teenagers. For small children, write about a small child's concerns.

LIKE A HANDSHAKE

Enclose a cover letter similar to the one on page 100 with your manuscript. This is a polite way of introducing yourself, like a handshake. Be brief and include only relevant information— the title of your piece, your age and grade (if the publisher wants to know that), other work of yours that has been published in a national publication, and prizes or awards received for your writing. *Don't* include facts such as your aunt Gwenn thinks you'll be the next Stephen King!

A publisher may ask for a query letter before you send your manuscript. Query letters are used to find out whether the subject matter of your manuscript would be of interest to the publisher. Tell the editor what your work is about. Give a simple summary of the subject or the plot in a single paragraph and any publishing credits you might have. A sample query letter is on page 101.

EXPLAIN YOUR IDEA

If you have an idea for a nonfiction book, you don't have to write the whole book before you present it to a publisher. You send a proposal telling the publisher about the book you want to write, giving him enough information to decide whether it's something he wants to publish. A cover letter explains your idea, whom it's for, how long you expect the book to be, whether there are any other books available that are similar to it, and when you plan to have it ready. A synopsis of the book, a table of contents, a brief one-paragraph summary of each chapter, and a couple of sample chapters make up the rest of the package.

Query letters and proposals may be sent to several publishers at the same time. Send your manuscript to one publisher at a time unless you read in the guidelines that it is okay to send *multiple submissions*. That means you can send the same manuscript to several publishers at the same time, as long as each of them accepts the practice. If yours is a multiple submission, say so in your cover letter, and if a publisher accepts your work, let the other publishers know right away that it is no longer available.

IF YOUR HAIR TURNS GRAY

Allow at least six to eight weeks for a response from a publisher; in some cases it could be shorter, in some cases longer. There's not much you can do about this, because it depends on the volume of manuscripts received by the publisher—so get to work on your next project to keep yourself from spending all your time wondering when that letter from the publisher will come. If you feel your hair is starting to turn gray, after three months or more, you can write to the publisher and ask if a decision has been made, but chances are this won't speed things up much. You can, however, ask to have your manuscript back if you don't want to wait any longer.

Some companies that call themselves publishers are really not, and after they tell you they like your work and want to publish it, they ask you for money. This is not the kind of publishing we're talking about. The publishers listed in this book are those who will publish your work either for nothing or who will pay *you* in money or copies of the magazine. Those who ask for money are called *subsidy publishers* (you subsidize, or help pay for, their costs) and should be avoided.

A rejection letter telling you the publisher cannot use your story or poem or article does not mean the end of the world. Sometimes very good writing gets turned down simply because the subject matter is similar to something else the editor has received, or it's just not grabbing that publisher. Perhaps it doesn't fit the image the publisher wants to convey. A story about hunting, for example, would not work well in a publication known for its strong position in favor of animal rights.

You May Have Something Special

If you get a rejection letter that is more than a form letter, it could be an indication that the editor thinks you have something special. If an editor asks you to send more of your work, be sure to note that and send other work to that publisher.

It's always a major disappointment to receive a rejection letter. It hurts, and you may even feel ashamed and not want to tell anyone. Even professional writers can't help having these feelings. Remember that it's not a rejection of you personally. Everything that goes on between you and a publisher has to do with your writing. If your writing does not fit the needs of a publisher, just try another publisher. They're all different, and each editor has his or her own tastes.

Even Dr. Seuss Got Rejections

Even well-known authors may have started out getting rejections. For example, Dr. Seuss, who wrote books you read when you were little, like *The Cat in the Hat* and *Green Eggs and Ham*, received dozens of rejections before finally being accepted. Rejection letters are part of the writing profession. Whether you like them or not (and I don't know anyone who does), you have to get used to them.

If you get a rejection letter and you're feeling down, think about why you want to be a writer:

- *You like sharing your ideas.*

- *You need to record your thoughts and experiences.*

- *You want a creative outlet for your feelings.*

- *You love working with words.*

- *You feel good when you write.*

- *You have stories you want to tell.*

- *Etc.*

Aren't those reasons still valid? Then why walk around as if your life has been shattered? Send your manuscript out again to another publisher. Meanwhile, start working on something else. It keeps you from chewing your nails waiting for the mail each day . . . and it keeps you producing fresh new work.

OCCASIONAL SETBACKS ARE NORMAL

There's no such thing as being a writer without experiencing an occasional setback. To be a writer, you have to learn to ride the waves: the high ones when someone likes your work or wants to publish something you've written, and the low ones when nobody seems to want to publish your work. Writers get tougher with experience.

LIKE WINNING A MILLION DOLLARS

If you can imagine someone knocking on your door to tell you you've won a million dollars, or a telephone call from the president inviting you to the White House for lunch, or being chosen as the most brilliant student in your school, you can imagine what it's like to have your manuscript accepted. You'll want to tell everyone you know. That kind of joy keeps most writers going, which is why they continue to send out their work despite the hard work and the rejection letters.

When your work is accepted for publication, you will be asked to sign an agreement allowing the publisher to publish your work. If you are under the legal age for signing contracts, a parent or guardian will have to sign it too.

Once you know your craft well and feel comfortable sending out your manuscripts and keeping track of them, you will know what it feels like, what it is, to be a writer. You have started on the journey but, as you have probably figured out, it's only a beginning. There's always something new to learn, or try, and always a new story to tell. That's why being a writer is always exciting.

Appendix A

Publishers Who Accept the Work of Young Writers

The publishers listed below feature young writers in their publications. Send for their guidelines; remember to enclose a SASE with your request. There are several market guides available that provide detailed information about publishers; only a few are devoted to markets for young people. The best of these are listed under Books, beginning on page 83. E-zines, or electronic magazines, accept work through e-mail and provide guidelines and sample issues online.

Blue Jean Magazine, for Teen Girls Who Dare, P.O. Box 90856, Rochester, NY 14609. Features interesting and exciting teen girls in action.

Boodle: By Kids, For Kids, P.O. Box 1049, Portland, IN 47371. Looking for humor, offbeat stories, and poems.

Creative Kids, Prufrock Press, P.O. Box 8813, Waco, TX 76714-8813. Publishes original poetry, stories, puzzles, games, editorials, reviews, and songs from young people ages eight to fourteen.

Cyberkids. One of the most popular online magazines featuring stories and artwork by kids. Publishes stories, articles, cartoons, jokes, and humorous essays for seven- to eleven-year-olds. Prefers illustrated work, but will consider unillustrated submissions. Needs nonfiction articles on topics of interest to young people from various parts of the world. (See their listing under Contests in Appendix B.) Also *Cyberteens* for older kids, twelve to sixteen. Web sites: http://www.cyberkids.com and http://www.mtlake.com/cyberteens

The Fudge Cake, P.O. Box 197, Citrus Heights, CA 95611-0197. Newsletter showcasing short stories and poetry from writers ages six to seventeen.

How On Earth! P.O. Box 339, Oxford, PA 19363-0339. Original writing by thirteen- to twenty-four-year-old readers that encourages critical thinking, creative expression, and activism concerning environmental, animal, and global issues.

Ink Blot, 901 Day Road, Saginaw, MI 48609. Newsletter for ages five to nineteen. Accepts nonfiction, essays, short stories, poetry, and acrostics.

Junior Editor, 709 SE 52nd Avenue, Ocala, FL 32671. Publishes short stories, poems, nonfiction, and essays by young writers from elementary grades through high school.

Just Kids Magazine, an E-zine: P.O. Box 152, Hawthorne, NV 89415, or e-mail: A2z48730 Run by a teenager, written by kids. Query about submissions of fiction, nonfiction, and poetry.

KidNews, an E-zine:
http://www.umassd.edu/SpecialPrograms/ISN/KidNews.html
E-mail: kidnews@massd.edu or dryan@umassd.edu or powens@umassd.edu Accepts stories, articles, reviews, features, profiles, newsy essays, editorials, columns, and letters for an opinion-editorial section.

Kids' Byline, P.O. Box 1838, Frederick, MD 21702. Accepts all kinds of writing by young people in grades 4 to 12; encourages letters to the editor.

Kid's Korner Newsletter, P.O. Box 413, Joaquin, TX 75954. A newsletter written for and by kids under eighteen. Publishes fiction and non-fiction.

Kids N' Sibs, 191 Whittier Road, Rochester, NY 14624l. Newsletter focusing on views and experiences of disabled children and siblings age twenty-one and under. No guidelines available, but send a SASE for a free sample.

Kids' World, 1300 Kicker Road, Tuscaloosa, AL 35404. Features poems, short stories—no horror—jokes, puzzles, games, and other material from young people up to age seventeen. The editor is a young writer herself.

Looking Glass Gazette, 909 N. Bellis, Stillwater, OK 74075-4304. E-mail: monty@cowboy.net Written entirely by kids up to eighth grade. The editor is a kid himself. Also available in electronic form. Accepts poems, articles, stories, jokes, riddles, puzzles, movie reviews, software reviews, letters to the editor, and requests for pen pals. You can sample an issue online free.

Marinara Sauce, 870 Chicago Avenue, Harrisonburg, VA 22801. E-mail: MarinaraS Written for and by young people from twelve to twenty, and edited by a teenager. Publishes poetry, short stories, editorials, work by guest columnists, and articles. Would like more light-hearted poetry, short stories with emotion, and humor.

The McGuffey Writer, P.O. Box 502, Oxford, OH 45056-0502. A literary journal featuring fiction, essays, poetry, personal experience stories, and essays written by kids from kindergarten through twelfth grade.

Merlyn's Pen, P.O. Box 1058, East Greenwich, RI 02818-0910. Phone 1-800-247-2027. Publishes one edition for grades 6 to 9, one for grades 9 to 12. Accepts stories, plays, essays, poems, reviews, word games, opinions, puzzles, and letters to the editor by young people in grades 6 to 12. Also publishes anthologies of stories originally published in the magazines.

MidLink Magazine, Caroline McCullen, Ligon GT Magnet Middle School, 706 E. Lenoir Street, Raleigh, NC 27601. An E-zine by and for kids ten to fifteen, linking middle-school kids all over the world through their art and writing. A sample issue is available online. Web sites: http://longwood.cs.ucf.edu/~MidLink and http://www2.ncsu.edu/ncsu/cep/ligon/ligon.home.html

New Moon, P.O. Box 3620, Duluth, MN 55803-3586. A magazine written and edited by girls eight to fourteen. Publishes profile articles of girls and women from the present and past and personal experience stories, opinion pieces, poetry, and short fiction, by and about girls.

Pandora's Box, E-mail: Akasha124@aol.com A bimonthly E-zine for ages twelve to twenty-two. Looking for short stories, columns, personal rantings and ravings, opinions, how-to's, articles, and poems. Now on the web at: http://pages.prodigy.com/PandorasBox/pandora.html

Prism, Lauderdale Publishing, 2455 E. Sunrise Boulevard, Ft. Lauderdale, FL 33304. Publishes writing and artwork by kids ages eleven to eighteen.

Shoe Tree, National Association of Young Writers, 215 Valle de Sol Drive, Santa Fe, NM 87501. A literary magazine by and for kids ages six to fourteen. Looking for stories, essays, book reviews, and poetry.

Skipping Stones, P.O. Box 3939, Eugene, OR 97403-0939. Accepts poems, stories, recipes, songs, games, book reviews, writings about your background, culture, celebrations, religion, interests, and experiences, by writers ages seven to eighteen. Writing may be submitted in any language and from any country.

Stone Soup, Children's Art Foundation, P.O. Box 83, Santa Cruz, CA 95063. Accepts stories, poems, personal experiences, and book reviews by children through age thirteen.

Tyketoon Young Authors Publishing Company, 7417 Douglas Lane, Fort Worth, TX 76180. Publishes fiction, nonfiction, and picture books in verse written and illustrated by students in grades 1 through 8. Illustrations must accompany every manuscript. Authors may collaborate with illustrators.

Wombat: A Journal of Young People's Writing and Art, 745 Prince Avenue, P.O. Box 8088, Athens, GA 30603. Publishes poetry, short stories, and nonfiction by kids ages six to sixteen.

Word Dance, Playful Productions, Inc., 59 Pavilions Drive, Manchester, CT 06040. For and by children from kindergarten through grade eight. Publishes poetry, fiction, and nonfiction.

The Writers' Slate, English Department, East Carolina University, Greenville, NC 27858-4353. Publishes fiction, nonfiction, and poetry written mostly by kindergarten through twelfth-grade students.

Writes of Passage USA, Inc., 817 Broadway, 6th Floor, New York, NY 10003. A national literary journal that publishes the writing of young people between the ages of twelve and nineteen in a biannual anthology. Submit up to five poems and/or two short stories at a time.

Young Adult Press, P.O. Box 21, Mound, MN 55364. A national tabloid written exclusively by kids between the ages of twelve and eighteen. Accepts fiction and nonfiction.

Young Author's Magazine, Regulus Communications, 3015 Woodsdale Boulevard, Lincoln, NE 68502-5053. Gives special attention to the learning disabled and at-risk students. Features fiction and poetry by children in elementary and secondary school.

Young Voices, P.O. Box 2321, Olympia, WA 98507. Publishes poetry, fiction, essays, and drawings by kids and teens ages six to eighteen. Looking for writers who are interested in writing feature articles and essays, as well as interviews with interesting people.

APPENDIX B

CONTESTS AND PRIZES

If you win or are a runner-up, your work will probably get published, and you may win other prizes as well. Write, or e-mail when appropriate, for entry forms. Be sure to include a self-addressed stamped envelope if you're using snail mail. Pay strict attention to the rules and follow them precisely; your entry can be eliminated if you don't. Only contests open to all young people nationwide, without entry fees, are included here, but a more detailed listing will be found in the market guides listed on page 85.

Ahmay Morgan Horse Literary Contest, P.O. Box 960, Shelburne, VT 05482-0960. Open to young people under age twenty-two. The contest judges poems and essays relating to a theme. Winners receive $25 and publication.

The Ann Arlys Bowler Poetry Prize, presented by *Read* magazine, is awarded each year. Students may submit up to three poems. Winners receive prizes and publication in *Read*'s all-student issue. Entry coupon may be obtained from Bowler Poetry Contest, Weekly Reader Corporation, 245 Long Hill Road, Middletown, CT 06457.

Creative Kids, P.O. Box 8813, Waco, TX 76714-8813. Has contests regularly on different themes. Winners receive prizes and recognition in the magazine. The contest entry form and rules can be found in the magazine.

Cricket League Contests, P.O. Box 300, Peru, IL 61354. Monthly contests in categories of art, poetry, short story, and photography for children up to age fourteen. Winners receive prizes, certificates, and publication in *Cricket* magazine.

Cyberkids (seven to eleven) and *Cyberteens* (twelve to sixteen) sponsor an international writing and art contest each year. The contest is posted on their web site in late August or early September: http://www.cyberkids.com and http://www.mtlake.com/cyberteens Prizes vary but have included a Macintosh computer. If you want to be included on the mailing list and do not have access to the Internet, call their toll-free number: 1-800-669-6574.

The Longmeadow Journal, c/o Rita and Robert Morton, 6750 Longmeadow Avenue, Lincolnwood, IL 60646. Sponsors annual short-story awards for writers between the ages of ten and nineteen. First prize is $175; second prize is $100. The top twenty stories are published in an anthology.

The Louisville Review Children's Corner Contest, Attn: Children's Corner, TLR, Dept. of English, 315 Humanities, University of Louisville, Louisville, KY 40292. Open to students in kindergarten through grade twelve. Winning entries may be published in *The Louisville Review*.

National Geographic World, 1145 17th and M Street NW, Washington, DC 20036-4688. Offers an annual geography-related writing contest for students in kindergarten through ninth grade.

National Written & Illustrated By . . . Awards Contest for Students, offered by Landmark Editions, Inc., 1402 Kansas Avenue, Kansas City, MO

64127. A contest seeking books written by kids ages six to nineteen. Each book must be written and illustrated by the same student. Contest winners receive publishing contracts, are paid royalties on book sales, and are given all-expense-paid trips to the publisher's offices in Kansas City, Missouri.

Paul A. Witty Outstanding Literature Award, c/o Cathy Collins Block, Ph.D., Professor of Education, Texas Christian University, P.O. Box 32925, Fort Worth, TX 76129. Prose and poetry are judged for three separate groups: elementary, junior high, and high school. Prizes: $25 and a plaque, and certificates of merit.

Publish-A-Book Contest, Raintree/Steck-Vaughn, P.O. Box 27010, Austin TX 78755. Open to students in grades 4 to 6, this annual contest is based on a theme. Winners receive $500 and a publishing contract.

Read Writing and Art Awards, Weekly Reader Corporation, 245 Long Hill Road, Middletown, CT 06457. Top winners are published in the All-Student Issue in April. First-place winners in each category receive $100; second-place, $75; third-place, $50. All winners and honorable mention recipients receive a certificate of excellence.

Seventeen Magazine/Dell Fiction Contest, Seventeen Magazine, 850 Third Avenue, New York, NY 10022. Awards for best short story by a writer age thirteen to nineteen. Cash prizes are given.

Spark! 1507 Dana Avenue, Cincinnati, OH 45207. Periodic writing and art contests for children from ages six to twelve.

Stella Wade Children's Fiction Award, AMELIA Magazine, 329 E Street, Bakersfield, CA 93304. Annual award for excellence in read-aloud stories for children. No entry fee for writers under seventeen, but entries must be signed by a parent, teacher, or guardian to verify originality. Prizes: $125 and publication in *AMELIA Magazine*.

"We Are Writers, Too!" Brigitta Geltrich, CWW Publications, P.O. Box 223226, Carmel, CA 93922. Annual contest for young writers

sponsored by *Creative With Words*. The one hundred top manuscripts are published.

The Writers' Workshop World Contest, Suite 212, The Flatiron Building, Battery Park Avenue, P.O. Box 696, Asheville, NC 28802. Annual national contest for children and teens, "Changing My World," with prizes for the best essay on a problem or issue they would like to change. There are two age categories: seven to twelve, and thirteen to eighteen.

The Writing Conference, P.O. Box 664, Ottawa, KS 66067. Writing contests in categories of poetry, narrative, or exposition on different topics each year, for students in grades 3 to 12. Winners receive a plaque and publication.

Young Playwrights Festival, Young Playwrights, Inc., 321 W. 44 Street, Suite 906, New York, NY 10036. Annual contest for writers up to age eighteen. Winners receive professional productions of their plays.

Young Playwrights Program, Very Special Arts, Education Office, John F. Kennedy Center for the Performing Arts, Washington, DC 20566. Contest judges plays about some aspect of disability, for students ages twelve to eighteen. The winner gets a trip to Washington to see his or her play produced at the Kennedy Center.

Appendix C

Books and Software

Books

Every writer must have a dictionary and a thesaurus; after that it's up to you. Add to your collection whenever you can. You can never have enough good reference material. If you can't buy the books you want, look for them in the library.

Writing

How to Write a Children's Book and Get It Published, Barbara Seuling. Scribner, 1991. Writing for children, from picture books to older fiction and nonfiction.

In Your Own Words: A Beginner's Guide to Writing, Sylvia Cassedy. Revised edition, Crowell, 1990. How to write all kinds of fiction and nonfiction, with an excellent section on writing poetry.

Putting It in Writing, Steve Otfinosky. Scholastic, 1993. The author shows different ways to organize nonfiction writing for school papers and reports.

Short Stories for Young People, George F. Stanley. Writer's Digest, 1986. The author shows how to plot short stories.

Thinking Like a Writer, Lou Willett Stanek. Random House, 1994. A writing guide filled with ideas to make writing more lively, plus writing exercises that are fun.

Time to Rhyme: A Rhyming Dictionary, Marvin Terban. Boyds Mills Press, 1994. An excellent resource for beginning poets, with many choices for rhyming words.

What If . . . ? Writing Exercises for Fiction Writers, Anne Bernays and Pamela Painter. HarperCollins, 1990. Exercises to sharpen your fiction skills and help you come up with new ideas.

What's Your Story? A Young Person's Guide to Writing Fiction, Marion Dane Bauer. Clarion, 1992. An award-winning writer shows you how to go from being a storyteller to a story writer in this guide to writing short stories.

Where Do You Get Your Ideas?, Sandy Asher. Walker, 1987. An upbeat book about the writing process, including poetry, plays, stories, and journals, with advice and exercises to inspire young writers.

Wild Words!, Sandy Asher. Walker, 1989. A lively book on how to "tame" words so they do what you want them to.

Writing in the Computer Age, Andrew Fluegelman and Jeremy Joan Hewes. Anchor Press/Doubleday, 1983. Includes guides for writing, editing, and formatting your work; electronic file-keeping; writing styles and strategies; editing and polishing your work; printing elegant manuscripts; information and file management; and networking.

Writing Your Own Plays: Creating, Adapting, Improvising, Carol Korty. Scribner, 1982. For grades six and up. A guide to many kinds of playwriting, from adapting a story that already exists to creating your own original work.

Young Person's Guide to Becoming a Writer, Janet E. Grant. Shoe Tree Press, 1991. This Canadian author and director of the International Young Authors' Camps coaches young writers on how to develop their writing abilities, and offers practical tips on money and rights.

Market Guides

The Market Guide for Young Writers: Where and How to Sell What You Write, 5th Edition, Kathy Henderson. Writer's Digest, 1995. This is an excellent guide to the markets available for young writers, offering a detailed listing of publishers known to accept submissions from writers eight to eighteen, plus contest information, editorial advice, articles, and essays by writers who were published when they were kids.

Rising Voices: A Guide to Young Writers' Resources. Poets & Writers, 1994. Lists magazines that publish work by young authors and national contests too, but is most helpful in its listings of resource centers around the country, state by state, and summer writing programs, conferences, and camps.

Young Authors' Guide to Publishers, Third Edition, Tracy E. Dils. Raspberry Publications, 1996. An excellent directory of book and magazine publishers, as well as contests, looking for manuscripts from young authors and artists. It includes practical advice, examples of cover letters and manuscript formats, and checklists to keep track of your work.

Other

Hey, Look . . . I Made a Book!, Betty Doty and Rebecca Meredith. Ten Speed Press, 1992. A step-by-step guide to creating your own bound books for your poems, stories, dreams, and journals, as well as for publishing multiple books.

Internet for Kids, Deneen Frazier. Sybex, 1995. Comes with software for NetCruiser, to gain instant access to the Internet. Covers Internet fundamentals and advises kids on getting around online. Packed with fun projects and great ideas, it has certain helpful features for kids interested in writing—communicating with published authors, using the Internet to get more information about a specific type of writing like playwriting, or looking up statistics.

Written & Illustrated by . . . , David Melton. Landmark Editions, 1985. Step-by-step instructions on how to write, illustrate, assemble, and bind your own books.

SOFTWARE

Lots of good software is available free (or for very little cost) on the Internet, so before you buy any expensive programs for writing, word processing, or getting around online to do research, check out what's available. Most computers come with a word processing program already installed—like Claris-works, or Microsoft Word. Even if yours doesn't, you can still write on your computer. Set it to "edit" mode, and you can do basic writing, making insertions and deletions, moving the cursor, and using the return key for new paragraphs.

If you do decide to get a commercial software program, there are several available. Broderbund has *The Amazing Writing Machine*, and The Learning Company has *Student Writer*, both of which have unique features that inspire creativity. There are other programs that are designed for use in schools, but which have features that might make them interesting for a dedicated writer in private use. Of these, I have certain favorites:

The Amazing Writing Machine, for grades 2 to 6, shows how to create letters, stories, poems, essays, and journal entries in an appealing, playful atmosphere. It is packed with clever tools to generate ideas, translate English into codes, find rhymes, etc. It's clearly a lot of fun—best for younger kids just learning to write in different forms. Broderbund Software, 1-800-521-6263.

Student Writing Center, for grades 4 to 12, combines word processing with desktop publishing applications. Features preformatted documents that include footnote, title page, and bibliography features; newsletter documents that feature masthead, multiple column options, and graphics; journal entries that feature dating and organizing; a bibliography maker, scalable graphics; and writing and grammar tips. The Learning Company, 1-800-852-2255.

Write On!, for grades K to 12. A series of literature-based writing activities designed to extend existing stories or to develop thinking and writing skills. Programs range from elementary to high school-age writers, from stories and poetry to journals and essays. Some programs are in Spanish. You probably won't find this in a software store, but check it out in their catalog. Humanities Software, 1-800-245-6737.

Writing Along the Oregon Trail, for grades 4 to 8. This fascinating program uses the background of the Oregon Trail for its writing activities, in which young writers assume the roles of pioneers. Another program that probably won't be on the shelves at your software store, but worth looking into. They don't have an 800 number, so send for their catalog by mail. MECC, 6160 Summit Drive North, Minneapolis, MN 55430-4003.

Key Words. I added this one in because some of you have a hard time typing your work because you don't know how to type properly. Through exercises based on interesting word patterns, this program teaches more effective use of the keyboard, building speed and accuracy—not bad skills for a writer to have. Humanities Software, 1-800-245-6737.

YOUNG WRITERS' CAMPS AND OTHER ACTIVITIES

CAMPS AND SUMMER PROGRAMS

Each program or camp has its own design and special features. Write for information and make comparisons. *Merlyn's Pen Magazine* features school and summer programs in the back of each issue; the February/March and April/May issues have more information than most. Advertising and sales director Kate Leach will answer your questions about any of these if you call her at their toll-free number, 1-800-247-2027.

Buck's Rock Camp, a summer camp for kids ages eleven to sixteen in New Milford, Connecticut, offers four- and eight-week sessions from late June through late August. Features story writing and poetry, and a publishing shop where student work is published. Write or call Jon Metric, 59 Buck's Rock Road, New Milford, CT 06776, 1-860-354-5030.

Carolina Friends Writing Camp, sponsored by the Carolina Friends School, a two-week concentrated writing experience for eleven- to fifteen-year-olds who like creative writing and want to improve their word processing skills. Contact Carolina Friends School, 4809 Friends School Road, Durham, NC 27705, 1-919-383-6602.

Center for Talented Youth, sponsored by Johns Hopkins University, is a three-week summer residential program for elementary, junior high, and high school students at different locations. All offer academic courses, including those in writing skills; some offer advanced writing classes. Contact Johns Hopkins University, 3400 N. Charles Street, Baltimore, MD 21218, 1-301-338-8427.

Duke Young Writers' Camp, for students in grades 6 to 11, blends traditional summer camp activities with a specialized writing program. Two-week sessions feature instruction, writing, and feedback in fiction, poetry, playwriting, journalism, and other areas from experienced writers and teachers. Contact Duke Young Writers' Camp, Summer Youth Program, Duke Continuing Education, Box 90702, Durham, NC 27708, 1-919-684-6259.

Elon College Center for Young Writers, offers creative workshops for students in grades 4 to 12, during the month of July. Workshops are in poetry and short-story writing. Contact Dr. John Hemphill, Elon College, Campus Box 2228, Elon College, NC 27244, 1-919-584-2353.

Interlochen Arts Camp, where students study music, dance, visual arts, creative writing, and theater arts. Contact Director of Admissions, Interlochen Center for the Arts, P.O. Box 199, Interlochen, MI 49643-0199, 1-616-276-7472, fax 1-616-276-7860.

International Young Authors' Camps, an international network of private camps designed to provide training for highly motivated young writers. Held on an annual basis for about one week in different locations around the world. Selection is based on a writing sample. Write to Janet Grant, Director of the Camps, c/o Free Spirit Publishing, 400 First Avenue North, Suite 616, Minneapolis, MN 55401, or call 1-612-338-2068.

Merlyn's Pen Mentors in Writing Program, a ten-week correspondence course for kids in fiction, nonfiction, or poetry, matches up a young writer with an editor. For more information call Kate Leach, advertising and sales director, at their toll-free number: 1-800-247-2027.

The Summer Institute for the Gifted, sponsored by Bryn Mawr College, George School, Vassar College, and Drew University, for students in grades 4 to 11. Features academic courses and creative participation programs. Contact College Gifted Programs, 120 Littleton Road, Suite 201, Parsippany, NJ 07054-1803, 1-201-334-6991.

University of North Carolina at Greensboro, presents a summer program (six-day sessions given in July and August) for children ages seven to fifteen, designed to give quality instruction in the arts and sciences. Students choose one major (two hours a day instruction) and two minors (one hour a day instruction) from over twenty classes, including creative writing. Contact Nora Reynolds, Associate Director, Continuing Education, UNC-Greensboro, 209 Forney Building, Greensboro, NC 27412, 1-910-334-5414.

Wofford College Summer Program, a two-week program for academically talented students in grades 5 through 9. Contact Wofford College, Spartanburg, SC 29303-3663, 1-803- 597-4500, fax 1-803-597-4549.

ONLINE EXPLORATIONS

There is exciting stuff going on online. There's the usual e-mail to communicate with other writers and friends, and the E-zines, or electronically produced magazines for young writers, but there are also places to chat with other writers, exchange writings, and invite guest authors to join you. Service providers like *Prodigy*, *America OnLine*, and *Compuserve*, all have areas just for writers. Once you find them, usually with the click of a button or by typing in a keyword like WRITERS, search further for places where young writers like to hang out. The following are only a few of those available, as new ones keep springing up all the time.

Ink, a writing club on *America OnLine* is for young people ages eleven to fourteen who want to get their work published. Meets weekly in a private room, has guest speakers, sponsors, and monthly contests. Members share their writing, and work may be published in the club newspaper, *Pen*. E-mail: Alexis4157@aol.com for information on joining and submitting work.

Inkspot, an exciting web site for writers, has a special area devoted to young people at: http://www.inkspot.com/~ohi/inkspot/young.html
Created by Debbie Ridpath Ohi, a children's book writer from Toronto, Canada, this site helps young writers find what they're looking for, guides them to reference works like dictionaries and thesauruses, shows them places on the net to get their writing published, offers writers' tips, provides information about specific kinds of writing (screenwriting, mysteries, etc.), and offers a free e-mail newsletter called *Inklings*.

The Internet Public Library: Youth Division is a virtual library where you can find reference material, book lists, interviews with writers, and a "Writing Page." Check it out: http://www.ipl.org/

The Quill Society is a fellowship of young writers between the ages of twelve and twenty-four with bright imaginations, and great stories to share. Membership includes weekly chats and reading of your work by at least two other members. Information and applications for membership can be obtained by going to their web page. E-mail:
Lewis Hyatt/hyatt@aimnet.com or
Hung Chia Yuan/hungcy@umich.edu

Owl (the On-Line Writing Lab at Purdue University) is designed to help older students write research and/or report papers. If you're writing a serious paper and have a specific problem with formatting, footnotes, bibliographies, etc., the OWL team will try to help you. In the subject line type: **owl-request** Type in your question, being as specific as possible, and send it e-mail to: **owl@sage.cc.purdue.edu** A tutor will reply within two to four days.

STATE PROGRAMS FOR YOUNG WRITERS

There are many regional programs—conferences, workshops, and festivals—for young writers. Many of them are listed in *Rising Voices* (see in Appendix C under Books: Market Guides, on page 85). Ask at your school or public library for information about programs offered in your state or nearby states. For example, the Oregon Council of Teachers of English in Portland sponsors an annual Oregon Writing Festival held in May, where young writers attend workshops, participate in a presentation from a published writer, and share their writing with other festival attendees. In Ohio, the Power of the Pen competition, held at Denison University in Granville, has young writers compete in three different writing exercises with members of a team. They are judged, and prizes (trophies, certificates, state-level scholarship money) are awarded to the best of each round, the best team, and the best individual writer. Check out what's happening in your state.

APPENDIX E

GLOSSARY OF TERMS
A WRITER SHOULD KNOW

browser software that helps you to find what you're looking for on the World Wide Web

character profile a detailed study of your character inside and out

conflict the struggle a character goes through in the development of a story

copyright legal protection for your writing to show it belongs to you

cover letter the letter you send to an editor with your manuscript

critique feedback on your writing from other writers, editors, or teachers

e-mail a means of communicating by computer with individuals or groups

exposition information that explains the background of your characters or story

E-zine an electronic magazine that is published online

first draft   the first time you write out your story or article completely

guidelines   a list of a publisher's requirements meant to help writers prepare their work properly

Internet   a vast computer network connecting people and resources all over the world electronically

marketing   finding the appropriate publishers for your work

multiple submissions   sending your work to more than one publisher at the same time

online   electronically connected to a network of computers

on speculation   to read without a commitment to publish

outline   a sketch or short version of your project, showing how the work progresses in steps

plagiarism   passing off someone else's words or ideas as your own

plot   the plan for your story

plotting   planning out the development of a story from beginning to end

proofreading   reading your work to check for errors

protagonist   the main character in your story

query   a letter to a publisher asking if they will consider your work

rejection letter   a letter telling you your work has not been accepted

revision   going over your work in order to improve it

royalties   payments made to authors for published work based on the number of copies sold

SASE   a self-addressed, stamped envelope

search engine   a software tool that is used to find something specific on the Internet

service provider   offers various services, usually including connection to the Internet

World Wide Web   a network of locations on the Internet

APPENDIX F
SAMPLES

Ima Goodwriter   About 1,200 words
203 Wordsmith Street
Prose Park, MA 01452
(123) 456-7890

How to Prepare Your Manuscript

by

Ima Goodwriter

This is where you begin the text of your manuscript. There should be lots of room above the title, and at least an inch of margin on both sides of the paper. Leave an inch and a half at the bottom of the page.*

Double-space the text. When you start a new paragraph, skip an extra space—that's actually *two* extra spaces. Be sure your type is dark—change your ribbon or cartridge if necessary.

*(Please keep in mind that this book measures only six by nine inches. You will be working on eight and a half by eleven inch paper.)

A sample manuscript page

On the following pages, use an abbreviated heading to identify your work.

Sending your work to a publisher is like going for a job interview. You want to look your best. Your manuscript should be clean and have no visible errors. If you make a correction, do it so it doesn't show, or do the page over.

These conventions about formatting help to make reading your manuscript, along with dozens, or even hundreds, of others, easier on an editor's eyes, and provide room for comments if necessary.

A sample manuscript page

203 Wordsmith Street
Prose Park, MA 01452
October 19, (year)

Noah Lotte, Editor
The Happy Reader Press
77 Windowseat Lane
Bookerville, MN 55118

Dear Mr. Lotte:

I am writing to you to request a copy of your guidelines for writers. I have enclosed a self-addressed, stamped envelope for your convenience.

Thank you. I look forward to hearing from you.

Sincerely,

Ima Goodwriter

Enclosure: SASE

A sample request for guidelines

203 Wordsmith Street
Prose Park, MA 01452
March 21, (year)

Noah Lotte, Editor
The Happy Reader Press
77 Windowseat Lane
Bookerville, MN 55118

Dear Mr. Lotte:

The enclosed manuscript, "A Porcupine Goes to School," is based on a visit by a wildlife expert to our school. The article is 1,000 words, and is for kids ages nine to twelve. I believe it will be of interest to your readers.

I am in the sixth grade at Prose Park Elementary School, and have been writing for two years. My work has appeared in the school newspaper, *The Prose Park Press,* and one of my poems was selected to represent our school in a Festival of the Arts Program here in Massachusetts.

I understand that you will be reading my manuscript on speculation. If you cannot use my article, please return it in the enclosed SASE. Thank you for taking the time to read my manuscript. I look forward to hearing from you.

Sincerely,

Ima Goodwriter

Enclosure: SASE

A sample cover letter. Adapt yours to suit your own work and background and the magazine you are submitting to.

203 Wordsmith Street
Prose Park, MA 01452
June 11, (year)

Noah Lotte, Editor
The Happy Reader Press
77 Windowseat Lane
Bookerville, MN 55118

Dear Mr. Lotte:

This summer I will be taking part in a two-week trip with the organization On Your Own, a group that encourages surviving on one's own in the wilderness. Each group of five teenagers is expected to survive on its own on an island with only a one-day supply of food and water. We will also take a rugged climb up Mount Traynor, go down the North River on a whitewater rafting trip, and set up camp in a remote area of Black Snake Canyon.

I have read your magazine and know that you publish personal experience adventures. I would like to know if you would be interested in considering my account of my wilderness adventure. I plan to keep a journal throughout my two weeks. My article will be completed by September 1.

I have been editor of my school newspaper and have had articles published in an online magazine, *Cyberteens*. Please let me know if my article would be of interest to you. I understand that my work would be submitted on speculation.

Sincerely,

Ima Goodwriter

Enclosure: SASE

A sample query letter.

A Writer's Stretching Exercises

If you want to stretch your writing muscles, here are a few writing exercises. Time yourself for five minutes—not more than that because then you start to fuss over your work. The idea is to write spontaneously, without planning . . . exactly the opposite of what you do when you're doing serious writing.

Matching Characters and Situations

Take a character from the first column and a situtation from the second column and put them together. Then write down an idea that uses both choices.

Characters	Situations
a grumpy old man	hogging a video game
a snob	going to the hospital emergency room
a rodeo cowboy	entering a creepy place
a timid young man	getting stuck in an elevator
an absent-minded person	being held hostage by a bank robber
a rowdy teenager	flying in a plane that's having engine trouble

a gangster	being plagued by a tagalong
a glamorous superstar	eating a strange vegetable
a smelly dog	getting on TV
a seven-year-old brat	hitting a ball though someone's window

WRITING DIALOGUE

1. Write a dialogue between a child and a grown-up, involving a snake.

2. Write a dialogue between two people stuck in an elevator together.

3. Write a dialogue between you and a friend after you've broken one of her treasures.

WRITING SCENES

1. Write a scene involving smelly sneakers.

2. Write a scene about something your brother does to tease you.

3. Write a scene about two people, both in a desperate hurry, trying to grab the same cab.

BRAINSTORMING

1. Go over what happened in your life today. Jot down the details, for example, you had to wait until your teenage sister finished with the bathroom before you could get in there in the morning, or you got a passing grade on that killer math test, or you had to eat artichokes for dinner. Find some situation in your notes and brainstorm it to find a story.

2. Find three possibilities for story ideas from these ten situations. Brainstorm the ideas. Summarize each one in twenty-five words or less.

- Getting your picture in the newspaper
- Driving a car in an emergency
- Getting stuck with a bratty kid
- Losing money you were holding for a group
- Finding an escaped convict in your garage
- Working at a job dressed as a clown
- Getting locked in a museum after closing time
- Winning a prize of a baby elephant
- Bungling an interview with a famous star
- Finding yourself drifting out to sea

3. Choose the idea you like the best and write a one-sentence summary of the plot.

An Opening Paragraph

Think of something you know a lot about—collecting baseball cards, a certain kind of music, mountain bikes, baby-sitting, trout fishing—and you'll have something you can write about. If you have been to a special place like Disneyland or a rock concert or Paris, you can probably write something about that. Write an opening paragraph for an article on any subject that would make the reader want to stay with it to find out more.

Choosing a Topic

1. Think of three subjects that fascinate you. They could be anything at all: Siamese twins, polyester, the Gold Rush, gorillas, armor. Write down your three subjects.

2. Look up the three subjects in whatever is most handy: an encyclopedia, an almanac, a textbook, an atlas, or *National Geographic* magazines. Jot down anything you can find, in brief notes. Pick the subject that appeals to you the most after this preliminary research is done.

3. Look up your choice of subject. This time you want a lot more information, and you want it from at least two sources. Go to the library or go on the Internet and find out what you can about it.

4. Find an aspect, or a part of, your subject, that would make a good article on its own.

5. Come up with a title for the article you would write, if you had to, on this subject.

COMPARISONS AND METAPHORS

1. Compare the item from column A with the item from column B.

A	B
a puppy	a new pair of shoes
a kite	a flower
an umbrella	sunrise
fingers	a waterfall
firecrackers	snow
a loud radio	playing basketball
jumping on a bed	singing
a glass of milk	a parrot
a dead cow	winter

2. Think of a metaphor for your favorite teacher.

WORDSMITHING

Find a more active or colorful word (or words) to replace each of these:

cereal	room	wash	ask
walked	saw	dog	child
paid	quiet	held	coughed
sat	throw	pushed	old
carried	took	breathing	ached

ESSAYS

1. Write an essay about annoying habits.

2. Write an essay about capital punishment.

3. Write an essay about "in" clothes and "out" clothes.

ARTICLES

1. Write an article about roller coasters.

2. Write an article about superstitions.

3. Write an article about a favorite sport.

STORIES

1. Write a story about a dare to stay out of trouble.

2. Write a story about switching places with someone.

3. Write a story about being accused of doing something you didn't do.

INDEX

ABOUT THE AUTHOR

Barbara Seuling was born and raised in Brooklyn, New York. She didn't know for many years that she was a writer. She spent a lot of time drawing, and becoming an artist for Walt Disney was her childhood ambition. Later, she worked as a children's book editor and published her first freaky fact book at that time. Since then she has written a lot more books, including *You Can't Eat Peanuts in Church and Other Little-Known Laws* and *The Teeny Tiny Woman*, and a book for grown-ups, *How to Write a Children's Book and Get It Published.*

Ms. Seuling is a member of the board of directors of the Society of Children's Book Writers and Illustrators and has won several awards for her distinguished contributions to children's books, including the Christopher Medal and the American Institute of Graphic Artists Award. She lives in two places: the city (New York) and the country (Vermont).